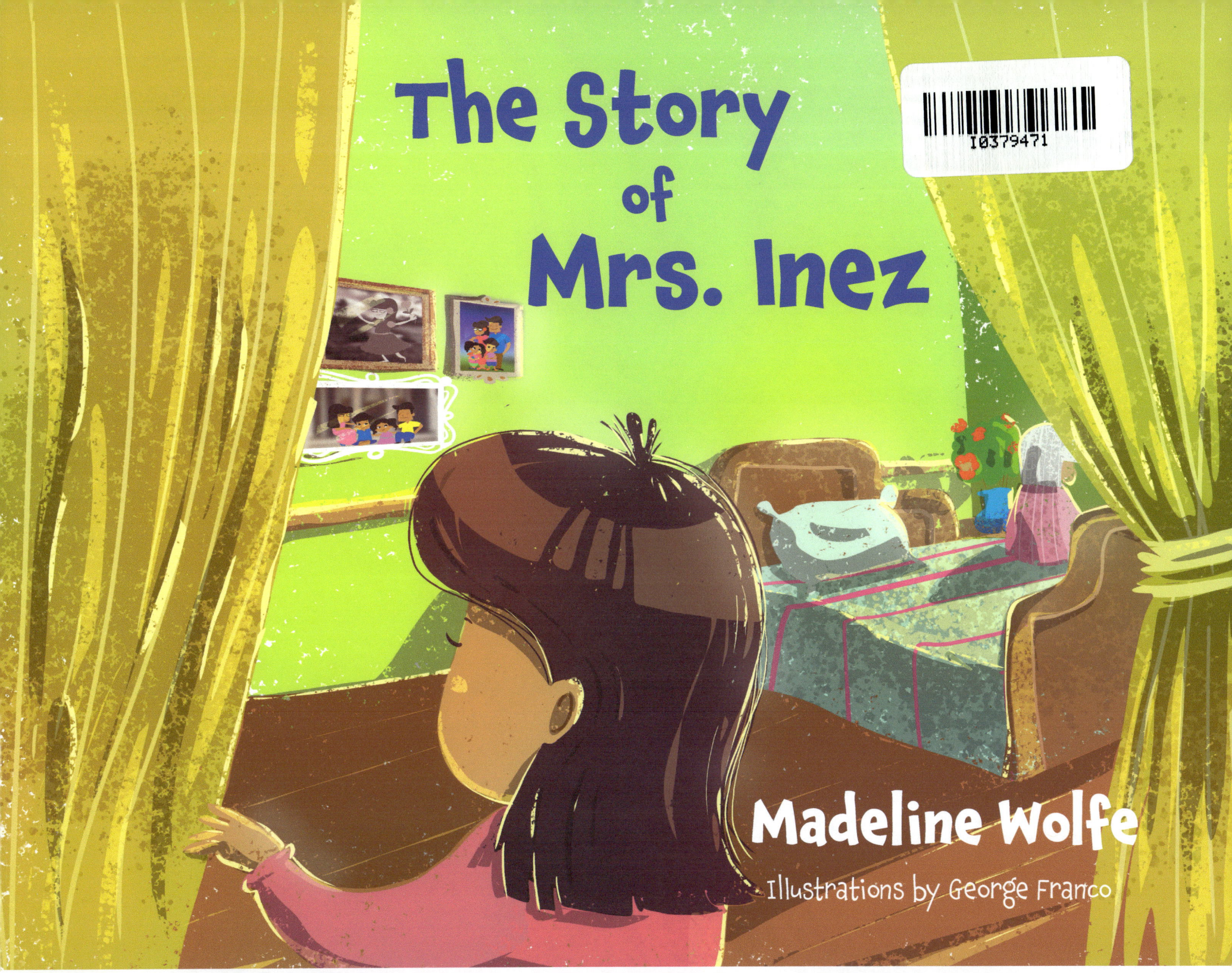

Copyright © 2019 Madeline Wolfe
ISBN: 978-1-940359-85-4
Library of Congress Control Number: 2019919162
Published in the United States of America

All rights reserved as permitted under the U. S. Copyright Act of 1976. No part of this publication may be reproduced, distributed, or transmitted in any form or by any means, or stored in a database or retrieval system, without the expressed written permission of the author and publisher.

Unless otherwise identified, all Scripture quotations have been taken from the NIV are taken from The Holy Bible, New International Version®, NIV®. Copyright © 1973, 1978, 1984, 2011 by Biblica, Inc.™

Illustrations by George Franco
www.georgefrancoart.weebly.com

Bedford, Texas
www.BurkhartBooks.com

# Storied Memory
## by Cassandra Livingston

Memories are planted within us
Stories help nurture the seed
Memories are visions of beauty
Stories help us to see

Memories are who we've been
Stories keep us all alive
Memories we take with us
Stories we pass down the line

When we share our stories
We share more than our past
We give a glimmer of us
Creating memories that last

Listen to the stories, child
Listen to them who speak
As they share the memories
They give you a piece to keep

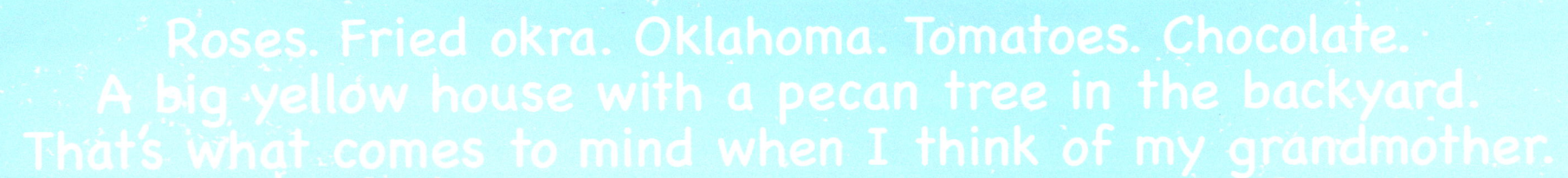

Roses. Fried okra. Oklahoma. Tomatoes. Chocolate.
A big yellow house with a pecan tree in the backyard.
That's what comes to mind when I think of my grandmother.

Sometimes we sit and talk in her room, and other times we find her in the cafeteria talking to the other residents.

I like when she's in the cafeteria.

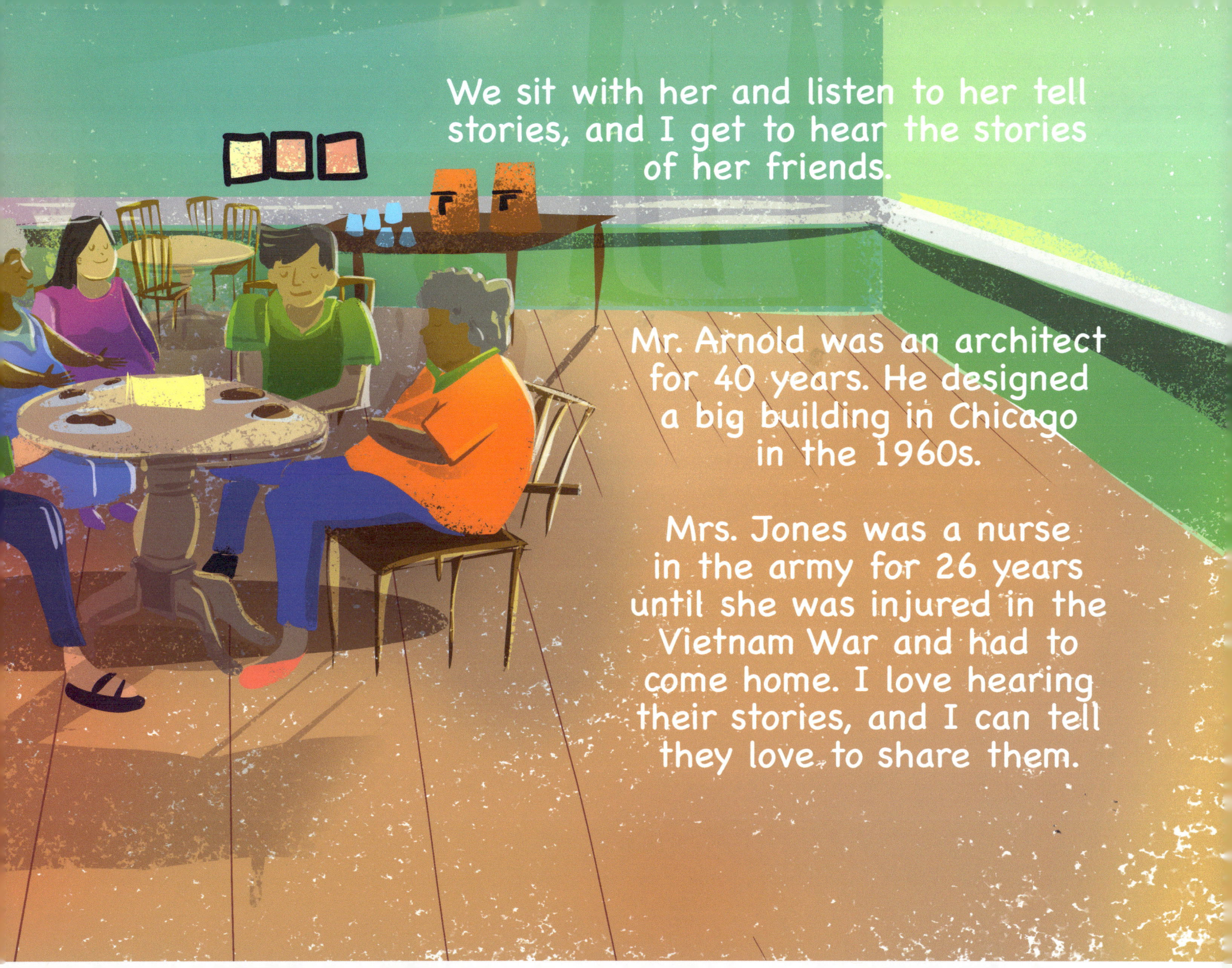

We sit with her and listen to her tell stories, and I get to hear the stories of her friends.

Mr. Arnold was an architect for 40 years. He designed a big building in Chicago in the 1960s.

Mrs. Jones was a nurse in the army for 26 years until she was injured in the Vietnam War and had to come home. I love hearing their stories, and I can tell they love to share them.

But my grandmother's stories are the best. It's my favorite part of our visit. I like her stories about what happened that week at Oak Grove, as well as those about the past. She talks about her life in Oklahoma.

How she had a well near her house where she got water. Or how her mother had a huge garden where they would get all of their vegetables and how she would stay up all night with her mom sewing blankets.

I especially enjoy the stories about my mom.
How she hated dresses and would always climb trees
and get dirty. My mom always smiles at those stories.
She looks like my grandmother when she smiles.

"Help me remember what?"
I ask every time.
The last time I asked that,
she looked at my mother
meaningfully before responding,

"They help you remember when I forget." I didn't know what that meant, but I didn't like the sad look in her eyes, so the next time she says that I'll just say "OK."

I try to do what my grandmother says
and keep the stories she tells,
so I write them down in my writing class.

It makes me smile to think of her
when she was young.
When she had long flowing brown hair
and wore pretty dresses.

I write them for me and for my mom, but most of all, I write them so my grandmother won't forget.

One Saturday, when we arrive at my grandmother's room, we notice she has a roommate. When we walk in, the curtain to her side is closed, so I can't see her. My grandmother says her name is Mrs. Inez.

My mom and grandmother begin to talk quietly, so I sneak over to the curtain. Mrs. Inez hasn't made a sound since we arrived. I peek around the curtain and see she is lying quietly in bed with her eyes closed.

I try not to move at all as I steal a glance at some of her pictures and wonder who everyone is. My mom notices me and tells me to let Mrs. Inez rest.

Each time we go back, I try to find out more about Mrs. Inez. Sometimes she's awake, but she doesn't talk. She sits at the edge of the bed and stares out the window. When my mom greets her, she doesn't seem to hear.

I can't help but look at her pictures. There's one with Mrs. Inez in a beautiful dress with flowers. It's a black-and-white photo like some of my grandmother's pictures. There are a couple of pictures with children, and I notice one of a bride and groom. I think it's Mrs. Inez, but I don't know for sure.

I ask my mom what she thinks about the pictures, and she tells me I'm being too nosy. "Everyone has stories," I say, repeating my grandmother's words. "I just want to know hers."

We arrive one day, and Mrs. Inez has company. My mother introduces us, and the woman says she is Mrs. Inez's daughter, Isabel. They chat for a little bit, then Isabel goes back to talking with Mrs. Inez. Mrs. Inez never responds, but she smiles shyly.

I want to know more about Mrs. Inez, so I work up the courage to ask Isabel about the pictures. "Is that Mrs. Inez in the wedding dress? When was that picture taken?

Who are the two kids in this picture? Did she grow up in Oklahoma, too?" My mom begins to tell me not to ask so many questions, but Isabel just laughs and says she would be happy to tell me about her mother.

It makes me sad that Mrs. Inez can't tell her own stories, but Isabel tells the story of her mom with so much energy, I can't stop listening. She smiles when she talks about how her mother always burned the chocolate chip cookies, and her eyes well up with tears when she talks about her brother who died of cancer six years ago.

Each story makes me wish I could talk to Mrs. Inez. I want to ask her more about her dog named Sammy, who Isabel said she had for thirteen years. I also want to ask her if she burned anything besides chocolate chip cookies.

In my writing class, I decide to write some of Mrs. Inez's story. I write about the chocolate chip cookies, and I draw her dog Sammy sitting by her feet like Isabel said he did every night. I hope that it's okay that I make him brown. I can't remember what color she said he was.

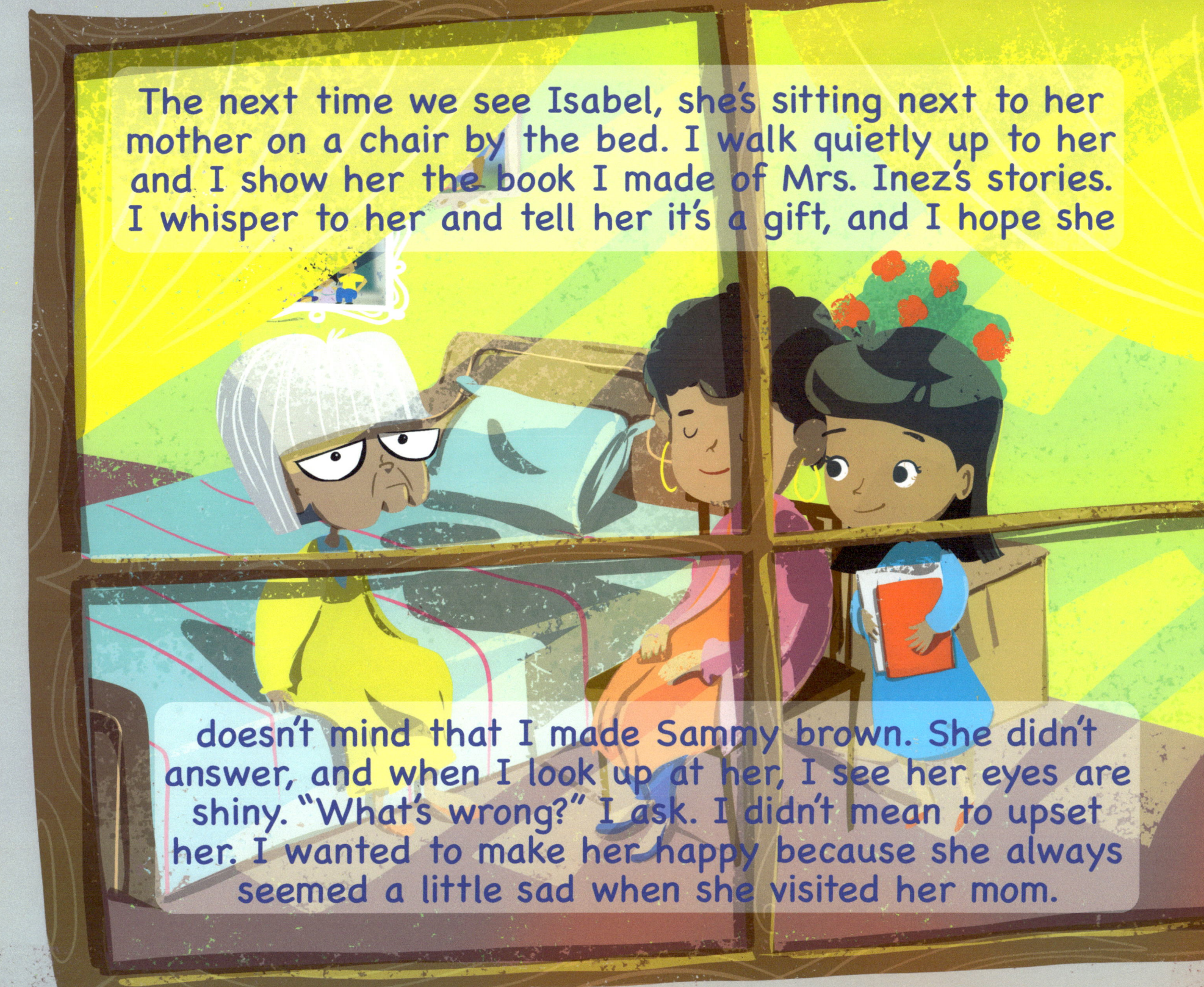

The next time we see Isabel, she's sitting next to her mother on a chair by the bed. I walk quietly up to her and I show her the book I made of Mrs. Inez's stories. I whisper to her and tell her it's a gift, and I hope she doesn't mind that I made Sammy brown. She didn't answer, and when I look up at her, I see her eyes are shiny. "What's wrong?" I ask. I didn't mean to upset her. I wanted to make her happy because she always seemed a little sad when she visited her mom.

"Nothing," she said. "Thank you so much. The book is beautiful." She thumbs through a couple of pages, and then says,

"You're a very good writer." I tell her I have lots of practice writing my grandmother's stories.

"You know, a lot of people ask me about my mother. The nurses always ask me questions. Do you mind if I leave the book right here on her table so other people can read it?"

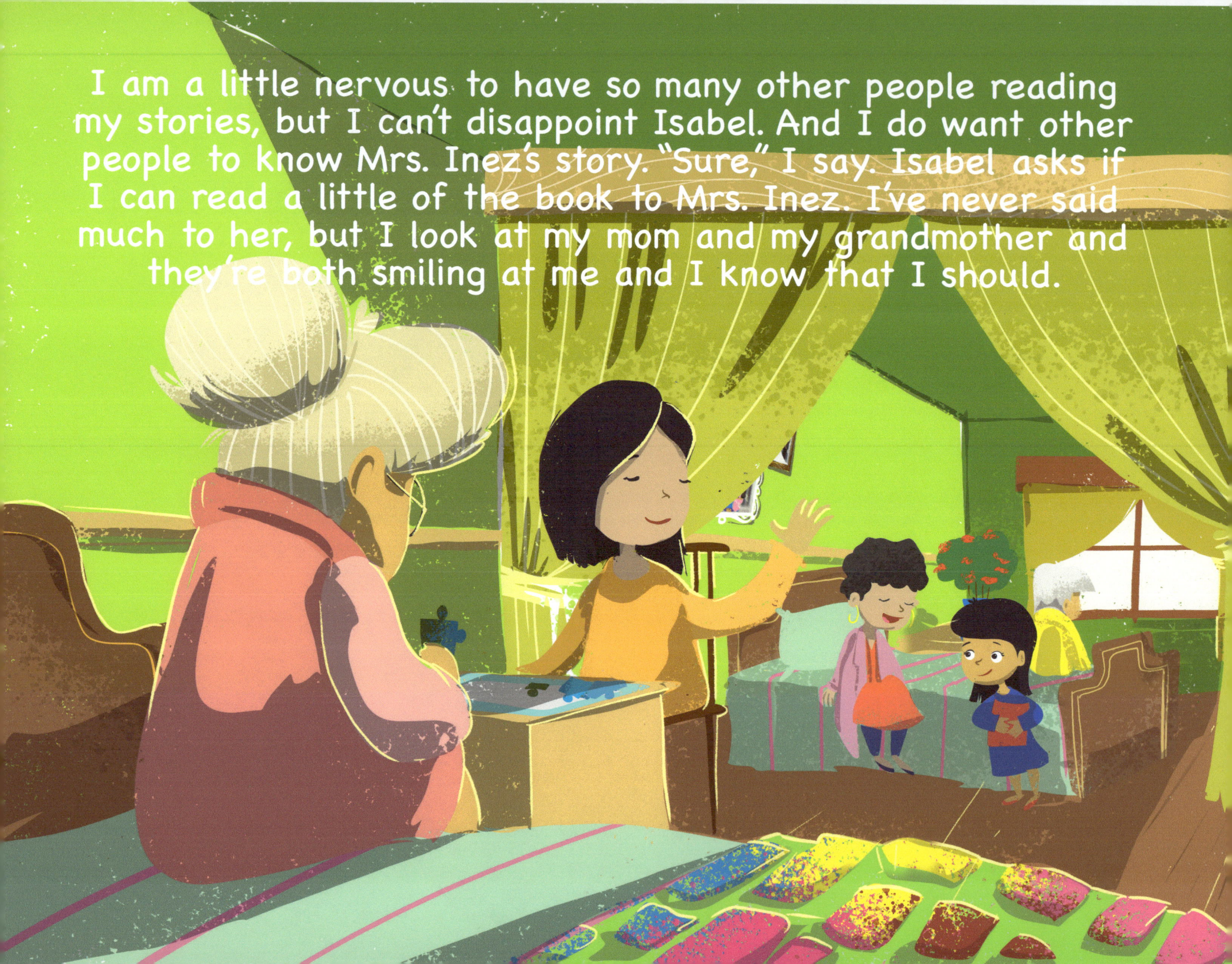

I am a little nervous to have so many other people reading my stories, but I can't disappoint Isabel. And I do want other people to know Mrs. Inez's story. "Sure," I say. Isabel asks if I can read a little of the book to Mrs. Inez. I've never said much to her, but I look at my mom and my grandmother and they're both smiling at me and I know that I should.

I sit in the chair Isabel was in, and I begin to read the story about the time she sewed a blanket for the neighbor's new baby and how Sammy stole it and wanted to keep it.

When I say Sammy's name, Mrs. Inez repeats, "Sammy." She smiles a little bit and looks at me. I keep reading the story and she keeps smiling. I'm glad that I can make her happy.

Now when I go back to see my grandmother, I always look over to see if the book is still there. I can see it's been read because the pages are starting to bend back. I hope Mrs. Inez reads it sometimes and smiles when she reads about her past. It also makes me smile to know that others will know the story of Mrs. Inez.

There are many people like Mrs. Inez.
As a result of Alzheimer's, people who once led vibrant, joy-filled lives end up needing around-the-clock care and assistance.

Alzheimer's is a disease that afflicts millions of people and those that love them. It affects the brain and causes memory loss and confusion. According to the Alzheimer's Association, the majority of people with this disease are over the age of 65. There is no cure, though there are treatment options available and research continues.

Learn more about Alzheimer's and support opportunities at alz.org.

## About the Author

Madeline Wolfe can be found somewhere in Texas surrounded by her family or with her nose stuck in a book. She absolutely adores her grandma, and she's a big fan of 90s music and planning her next vacation. As a former teacher, she knows how important it is for little ones to understand the stories of others.

www.ingramcontent.com/pod-product-compliance
Lightning Source LLC
Chambersburg PA
CBHW042110090526

44592CB00004B/68